First published in
North America by Annick Press 2005
Text © 2003 Meg Clibbon
Illustrations © 2003 Lucy Clibbon
Originally published by Zero to Ten Limited
(a member of the Evans Publishing Group)
© 2003 Zero to Ten Limited

Cataloging in Publication
Clibbon, Meg
Imagine you're a princess! / Princess Megerella, Princess LuluBelle.
(Imagine this! series)
ISBN 1-55037-921-6 (bound).—ISBN 1-55037-920-8 (pbk.)
1. Princesses—Juvenile literature. I. Clibbon, Lucy II. Title.
III. Series: Clibbon, Meg Imagine this! series.
GT5390.C55 2005   j940.1'086'21
C2005-901407-5

Distributed in Canada and the U.S.A. by Firefly Books Ltd.
www.annickpress.com
Printed in China

Imagine you're a
Princess!

Princess Megerella

does not have tiny feet in glass slippers, or an ugly sister but she did marry her Prince Charming, long, long ago and still lives happily ever after. She dreams of turrets, velvety lawns and peacocks but is quite happy with chimney pots, a backyard and sparrows.

Princess Lulubelle

Princess Lulubelle works in an enchanted studio in a fairytale land full of fun-loving princesses and charming princes. In her spare time she is to be found singing and dancing the night away at palace parties, or tending to her two pet unicorns at the bottom of her garden.

We would like to dedicate this book to two charming and adorable Princesses,

Katie and Molly

What is a Princess?

Definition:

A princess is someone who is the daughter of a royal family or who is married to a prince. Anyone can be a princess if they feel like one, or behave like one.
So the world is full of princesses.

What Do Princesses Look Like?

Everybody knows what a princess in a fairy tale is supposed to look like.

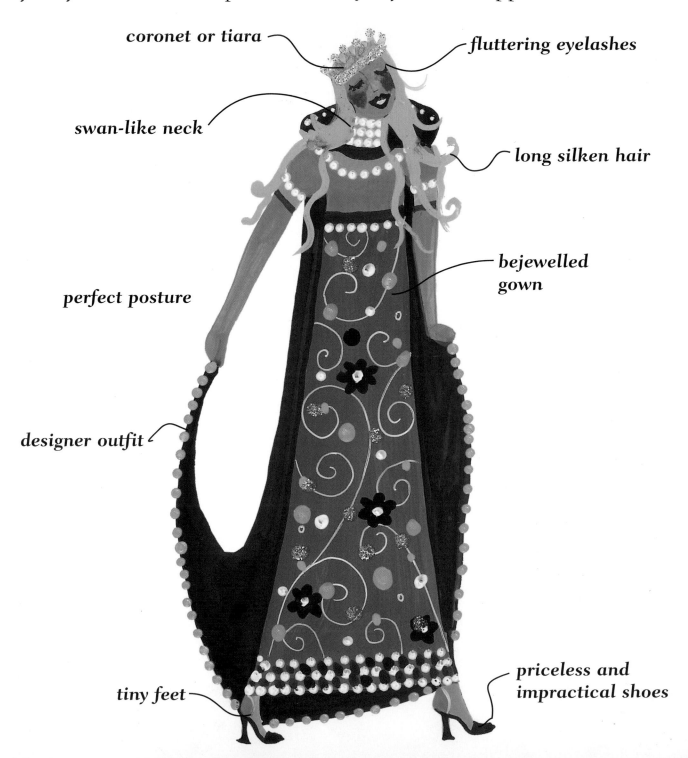

coronet or tiara

fluttering eyelashes

swan-like neck

long silken hair

bejewelled gown

perfect posture

designer outfit

priceless and impractical shoes

tiny feet

However, princesses often look a lot like you and me and don't usually have fairy tales written about them.

If you want to be a special princess you can use your imagination, close your eyes and go into the land of dreams.

Where Do Princesses Live?

Princesses live in royal palaces or beautiful fairy-tale castles with tapering turrets and tall walls. Velvety lawns and perfumed gardens are laid out between shady trees and sparkling fountains, where the princesses can walk and play games. The rooms in the castle are hung with brocades and tapestries, and everywhere there are precious objects and sumptuous furniture. Soldiers guard the princesses from harm and servants make their lives easy and carefree.

The Bedroom of a Princess

It is said that some princesses are so delicate and sensitive that they can feel the slightest wrinkle in their bed. Every night a lady-in-waiting checks that there are no lumps in the bed or peas* under the mattress, and then smoothes the silken sheets. Modern princesses have duvets and make their own beds, but it is still a good idea to check for peas, chips, and popcorn.

*Read the story of *The Princess and the Pea*

Another servant brushes the princess's hair a hundred times with a soft brush. Musical instruments play gently to send her to sleep and the air is filled with sweet fragrances. Outside her window a nightingale sings and the princess dreams delightful dreams.

Pretty Princess Things

Here is a peep at some of the hundreds of clothes, shoes, jewels, and accessories that belong to a princess. Her ladies-in-waiting have a very demanding job looking after all these pretty things.

Princess Pets

Princesses love animals and birds, but only if they are friendly, clean, and, of course, very well trained. Swans, butterflies, peacocks, and song birds are popular but their favorites are unicorns. These are magical, mystical creatures which are only glimpsed by special people such as princesses.

Becoming a Princess
a Step-by-Step Guide

1. Find the clothes that suit you best. Ask the queen (your mother) if you can swap clothes with friends.

2. Eat good, healthy food and drink lots of water. Your well-being will benefit.

3. Dancing is the best exercise for a princess. Walking the royal dogs is good but riding a unicorn is even better.

4. Remember never to neglect your personal grooming. Princesses always have shiny hair, clean nails, and gleaming teeth.

5. When speaking, choose your words with care. It's probably best not to shout or use vulgar language.

6. Think beautiful thoughts. These will show in your face, and you will be a delight to everyone around you.

...Of course, you will make everyone very jealous – but this is one of the penalties of being a beautiful princess.

Diary of a Princess

Monday:
Had a terrible night. Woke up black-and-blue with bruises from a crumb the chambermaid had left in the bed.

Tuesday:
Awoke early and went to the palace gym for posture practice and dancing lessons. Returned to my bedroom for manicure and hair treatment. Dressed in my silk morning dress and played croquet with the Prince of Tarnia. Declined his marriage proposal.

Wednesday:
Launched a ship.

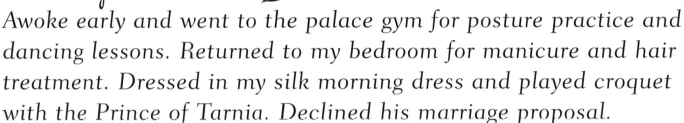

Thursday:
Attended a medal ceremony for several knights who had rescued damsels in distress. Later had to be very charming to them all at the state banquet. I think they may wish to marry me. I will decline, of course.

Friday: Spent all day with my dress designer. Went to bed early quite exhausted.

Saturday:
Walked in the garden. Rested in the afternoon. This evening we had a wonderful party in the palace. I wore some new jewels and my favorite ballgown with the matching tiara. My dancing went well, and everyone was entranced. Went to bed very late but happy.

Sunday:
Rested.

Dating Agency

Of course all the princes, knights, and pirates for miles around want to marry one of these wonderful princesses, but princesses have to be very choosy. There is such a shortage of suitable princes and eligible bachelors that an enterprising Fairy Godmother has started a Royal Dating Agency. Here are two of the advertisements.

Wanted

Prince for lovely and talented Princess. Must enjoy picking pretty flowers. Must be very good-looking and not rough and nasty. Must be prepared to be in constant attendance on Princess and give up horrid hobbies like football and fighting.

I'm afraid I don't match the requirements of this spoiled princess. No thanks.

PRINCE PARAGON

Wanted

Prince (or Pirate) for bored Princess. Need not be handsome. Preferably someone with a motorbike who can take her off on adventures. Should be fun-loving and prepared to experience the real world together.

I must arrange a meeting immediately with this adorable creature. Yes please!

PRINCE PARAGON

Essential Life Skills

It is most important that princesses are charming all the time, even if they don't really feel like it. Here are some examples of charming behavior:

1. Always greet parents graciously in the morning.

2. Offer to help others.

3. Be fascinating and interesting at banquets and princess parties.

Etiquette

These are some of the rules of social behavior which few people bother with today except princesses.

1. *Always wear your crown on formal occasions.*

2. *Never enter a room after other people – always go first. (Except for trumpeters.)*

3. *Always be polite and pay attention to people, otherwise they will think you are snobbish.*

4. *Only wear sneakers with cotton or wool, never with silk or satin.*

5. *Don't shout.*

7. *Don't flick peas at mealtimes.*

8. *Never get angry in pajamas.*

9. *Always carry a clean handkerchief – especially if you intend dropping it for a prince to pick up.*

Princesses adore giving lavish parties like this one...

1. Grand entrance staircase
2. Banquet room
3. Fizzy drinks fountain
4. Fanfare trumpeters
5. Musical statues
6. Pass the parcel
7. Courtly dancing
8. Court jester
9. Royal gifts

Famous Princesses

Despite all the advantages, princesses in stories always seem to be getting into some sort of trouble. This is generally because they are so beautiful. Being beautiful has its drawbacks. Princess Snow White made her evil stepmother jealous and Princess Sleeping Beauty, through no fault of her own, upset her godmother. Rapunzel, who ended up as a Princess but started off as an ordinary girl with extraordinary hair due to her mother eating a lot of cabbage, was shut up at the top of a tall tower by a witch. It was only because brave and handsome princes went to a lot of inconvenience to rescue them, that they survived at all, but of course they did, and they all lived happily ever after.

Princess Language

Princesses never use ugly words.
They are taught gracious phrases at Charm School.
Practice these on your friends and family.

"Good morning, dearest mother and father,
Did you sleep well?"

"Sadly, I must decline your gracious
proposal of marriage."

"Pray accompany me into yonder garden."

"How sweet of you to risk
your life on my behalf."

Things to do

Princess Painting

Paint a picture of a fairytale princess
in beautiful gardens. Use lots of
lovely bright colors and use
glitter, stickers, and pressed
flowers for finishing touches.

Pressed Flowers

Collect small flowers, pretty leaves, and grasses.
Spread them out carefully between sheets of newspaper or
paper towel. Put heavy books or weights on top for several
weeks until they are dry. Then you can arrange your
pressed flowers on cards or pictures to give to members of
your family, or ladies-in-waiting
or your favorite prince . . .

Princess Tea Party

Arrange a party for all your friends,
with special games, drinks and food,
for example Maids-of-Honour cakes.

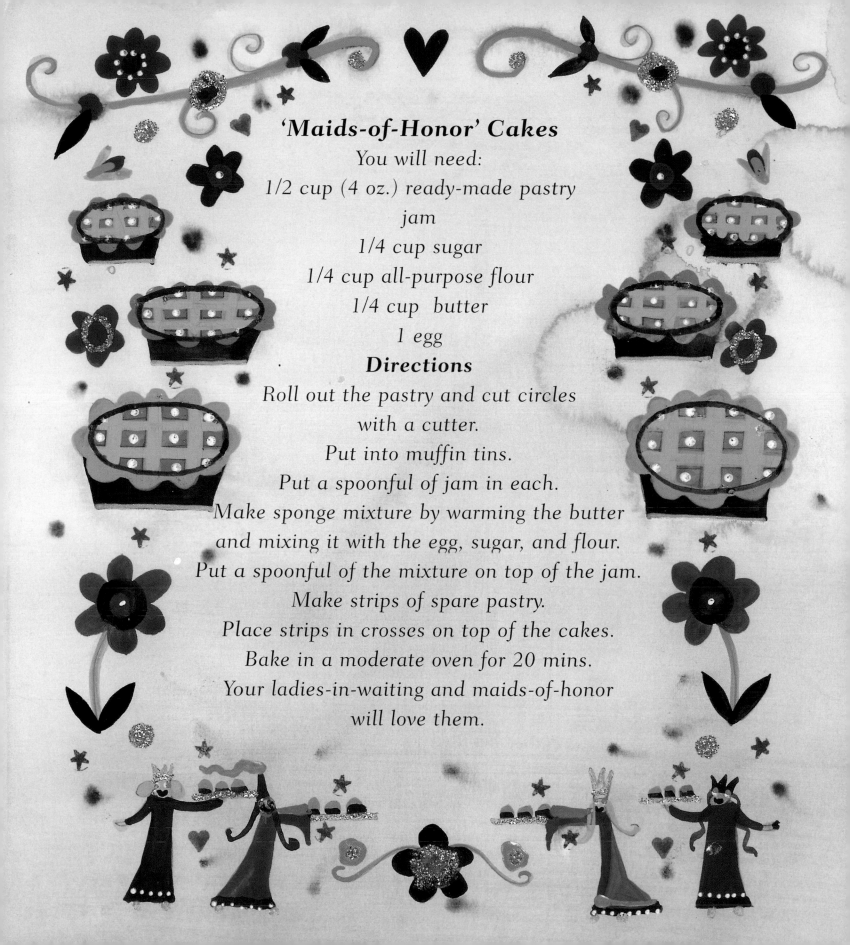

'Maids-of-Honor' Cakes

You will need:

1/2 cup (4 oz.) ready-made pastry

jam

1/4 cup sugar

1/4 cup all-purpose flour

1/4 cup butter

1 egg

Directions

Roll out the pastry and cut circles
with a cutter.
Put into muffin tins.
Put a spoonful of jam in each.
Make sponge mixture by warming the butter
and mixing it with the egg, sugar, and flour.
Put a spoonful of the mixture on top of the jam.
Make strips of spare pastry.
Place strips in crosses on top of the cakes.
Bake in a moderate oven for 20 mins.
Your ladies-in-waiting and maids-of-honor
will love them.